SOPRANO

CONTEMPORARY THEATRE SONGS

SONGS FROM THE 21ST CENTURY

ISBN 978-1-4950-7152-2

HAL•LEONARD®

7777 W. BLUEMOUND RD. P.O. BOX 13819 MILWAUKEE, WI 53213

Visit Hal Leonard Online at
www.halleonard.com

PREFACE TO THE SOPRANO EDITION

A musical theatre soprano in the twenty-first century is often asked to sing material that is in a style and range that includes belting. It can be tricky deciding which songs are fundamentally intended purely for belting, and thus in the Belter volume of this series, and which songs are for a soprano voice that belts.

The songs from *Waitress* are a good example. If you listen to the cast album, it's apparent that Jessie Mueller is a soprano who also has a strong belt. Many theatre sopranos not only belt at times, but also sing in a vocal mix of belt and head voice that leans more soprano than belter/mezzo-soprano in its tone, timbre and color. Songs approached this way also fall in this soprano volume.

—The Editors

ABOUT THE SONGS AND SHOWS

THE ADDAMS FAMILY *(Broadway 2011)*
Music and Lyrics by Andrew Lippa

Charles Addams' *The Addams Family* cartoons, which debuted in *The New Yorker* in 1938 and ran periodically until Addams' death in 1988, satirized the ideal American family by depicting a family of gruesomely ghoulish characters who take pleasure in things macabre. The musical revolves around a dinner date at the Addams' house with the family of Wednesday's boyfriend (and soon to be announced fiancé), a "normal" boy named Lucas Beineke. Wackiness ensues as the seemingly incompatible Addams and Beinekes try to get through the evening together. Pugsly, worried that he is losing his sister to Lucas, plans to drop a potion into her drink at dinner that would cause her behavior to become malevolent. However, near the end of Act I Lucas' mother Alice mistakenly drinks the potion instead. Under its influence she becomes inappropriate in front of everyone and sings **"Waiting,"** in which she laments the misery she feels in her passionless marriage.

AMAZING GRACE *(Broadway 2015)*
Music and Lyrics by Christopher Smith

The musical *Amazing Grace* tells of the dramatic life of John Newton (1725–1807), the man who wrote the words to the popular hymn of the show's title. Forced into the British Navy, Newton falls into the ocean during battle, is captured and imprisoned in Sierra Leone. Singer and abolitionist activist Mary Catlett assumes her friend and secret love is dead. She grieves in **"Tell Me Why."** John is able to stay alive by advising his captor Princess Peyai on how to better run her slave-trading empire. The Princess sends a ransom note to John's estranged father, the captain of a slave-trading ship. The captain immediately sails to Sierra Leone with a letter from the eager Mary. The captain is fatally wounded and dies, leaving John in command of the ship. John finds the letter from Mary in his father's coat. He hears her voice as he reads in **"I Still Believe,"** which inspires John to reevaluate his role in human trafficking. He eventually gives up this life, weds Mary, and joins her in fighting for abolitionism.

BIG FISH *(Broadway 2013)*
Music and Lyrics by Andrew Lippa

The big-hearted musical *Big Fish* is based on the original 1998 novel by Daniel Wallace, as well as the 2003 film adaptation by John August (who also wrote the book for the musical). The main characters are Edward Bloom, his wife Sandra and their son William. Edward has spent his life regaling Will with fanciful tales of his past, including a story about a giant fish that jumped into a man's arms after Edward taught the fisherman to catch fish by doing the "Alabama Stomp." Scenes jump between the present and the past, interspersed with Edward's fanciful tales. Edward becomes seriously ill with cancer. The adult Will returns home and in conversation with his mother, she describes her relationship with her husband and son in **"Two Men in My Life."** As Edward's condition worsens, he tells Sandra that the roof of their house should last another ten years after his death. She sings the emotional and touching **"I Don't Need a Roof"** in response. By Edward's funeral, Will has learned that all of his father's tales were in fact based in truth.

THE BRIDGES OF MADISON COUNTY *(Broadway 2014)*
Music and Lyrics by Jason Robert Brown

The Bridges of Madison County tells the story of an Italian immigrant "war bride," Francesca, on a farm near Winterset, Iowa, in 1965. She sings **"To Build a Home"** at the top of the show about her mundane life. While her husband and children are away at a 4-H fair, a *National Geographic* photographer, on assignment to shoot the historical covered bridges of the county, knocks on her door asking for directions. The photographer, Robert, and Francesca have an almost immediate connection that results in a brief but intense affair. Francesca sings **"What Do You Call a Man Like That?"** soon after meeting Robert as she begins to notice a special spark between them. Francesca and Robert fall deeply in love. Many years pass. Francesca's husband dies. She was never again in contact with Robert, who waited for her call his entire life. Francesca finally receives a letter that informs her of his death. In **"Always Better,"** Francesca sings of the circumstances and love that brought her together with Robert, of the choice she made to remain with her husband and children, and of the abundance of love she has had in her life. The musical is based on the 1993 novel of the same name by Robert James Waller. A film version was released in 1995, starring Meryl Streep and Clint Eastwood.

DARLING
Music and Lyrics by Ryan Scott Oliver

Darling features a book, music and lyrics by Ryan Scott Oliver and was conceived by Brett Ryback. From the composer-lyricist's website: "*Darling* is a dark deconstruction of J.M. Barrie's Peter Pan, following a girl called Darling in a 1920's New England dreamscape who is swept away by Peter, a rent-boy. When she loses herself in the seedy underground of jazz, sex and a mysterious white powder called Dust, can the lost girl find herself again?" In **"The View from Here"** 16-year-old Ursula Morgan sits on her windowsill, reflecting on her neglected childhood and hopeful for a better future. Though not produced in Off-Broadway or Broadway as of this writing, *Darling* is the winner of the Boston Metropolitan Opera Mainstage Award, the Pace New Musicals Award, the Weston Playhouse New Musicals Award, and the Jonathan Larson Grant for Ryan Scott Oliver. In 2010 *Darling* was featured on the "Bound for Broadway" episodes of the television show *The Apprentice*.

DEATH TAKES A HOLIDAY *(Off-Broadway 2011)*
Music and Lyrics by Maury Yeston

Death Takes a Holiday is based on the 1924 Italian play *La Morte in Vacanza* by Alberto Casella. Its subject is death taking human form to understand what it means to be human, including all of the emotions that go along with it, such as love and fear. Death disguises himself as the recently deceased Prince Nikolai Sirki of Russia and stays at the home of Duke Vittorio Lamberti for the weekend, falling in love with his daughter Grazia. An English-language version of the play ran on Broadway in 1929. In 1934 the play was made into a film, and in 1998 it was remade into *Meet Joe Black*, starring Brad Pitt. *Death Takes a Holiday* was produced by the Roundabout Theatre Company and ran for three months in 2011. Grazia sings **"How Will I Know?"** as she realizes something has changed about her. At the end of the show Grazia and Death have fallen in love and touch, and she dies instantly. The two walk in death together as the curtain falls.

DIRTY ROTTEN SCOUNDRELS *(Broadway 2005; London 2014)*
Music and Lyrics by David Yazbek

Dirty Rotten Scoundrels is based on the 1988 film starring Michael Caine and Steve Martin, which itself was a remake of the 1964 film *Bedtime Story*. Two independent con men prey upon lonely, wealthy women vacationing on the French Riviera. The suave, British Lawrence Jameson poses as a rich, deposed prince who needs funds to fight revolutionaries. Crass American Freddy Benson tries to usurp fortunes through a sob story. The two grifters decide that the small town on the French Riviera isn't big enough for both of them. They choose a mark, Christine Colgate, the "American Soap Queen." Whoever gets to her money first will get to remain in town. In the end, after many double-crosses, Christine swindles them both. **"Nothing Is Too Wonderful to Be True"** is sung near the end of Act I, after Freddy tells Christine that he has lost the use of his legs and his only hope is $50,000 treatment from Dr. Emil Shüffhausen in Vienna. Christine is touched (or she pretends she is) and promises to help him. Freddy can't believe it, and she sings to assure him. Christine sings the "straight" version of the song, then Freddy adds a more wisecracking version before they briefly sing together at the end. The song has been adapted as a solo for Christine in this edition.

EVER AFTER *(2015)*
Music by Zina Goldrich
Lyrics by Marcy Heisler

Ever After received its world premiere in 2015 at the Paper Mill Playhouse, a major regional theater in Milburn, New Jersey, just across the river from Manhattan. The musical, based on the 1998 film starring Drew Barrymore, is a retelling of the classic Cinderella story, this time with a more empowered heroine. As in the traditional story, Danielle (the Cinderella character) is left with her cruel stepmother and stepsister following her father's death. In **"I Remember,"** surrounded by so many books at the monastery, Danielle is taken back to her childhood, sharing her memories of her beloved father.

FAR FROM HEAVEN *(Off-Broadway 2013)*
Music by Scott Frankel
Lyrics by Michael Korie

The musical *Far from Heaven* is based on a 2002 film directed by Todd Haynes. Set in suburban Connecticut in 1957, Cathy Whitaker is a housewife married to a successful advertising executive, Frank. Their life seems perfect, but she discovers that Frank is a closeted homosexual. As her life and relationship to her husband begins to unravel, Cathy seeks consolation in the friendship of Raymond, an African-American man who works as her gardener, and causes much gossip in doing so. The story deals with issues of gender roles, sexuality, race and the consequences of social taboos on people's lives in the conservative 1950s. **"Heaven Knows,"** the last song in the score, is hopeful. Cathy looks forward to the unknown adventures of life ahead, concluding that reality, despite its difficulties, is richer and more rewarding than delusional dreams. Kelli O'Hara played the role of Cathy in a limited run at Playwrights Horizons in 2013, and recorded the cast album, with Steven Pasquale as Frank.

FINDING NEVERLAND *(Broadway 2015)*
Music and Lyrics by Gary Barlow and Eliot Kennedy

Finding Neverland tells the same story as the 2004 film about the playwright J. M. Barrie, his developing relationship with his neighbors, and subsequent production of the play *Peter Pan* inspired by these interactions. First begun in the UK in 2012, the show went through major changes before its 2015 Broadway opening. The character of Sylvia Llewelyn Davies, a close friend to Barrie, was mother to boys who inspired the Peter Pan story. After her husband's death in 1907 and her own death in 1910, Barrie financially supported Davies' children. In Act I the ill Sylvia sings to her mother, Mrs. du Maurier about her concern for her boys and how Barrie comforts and assures her in **"All That Matters,"** deciding that she can only live for today. In **"Sylvia's Lullaby"** she soothingly sings to her children.

A GENTLEMAN'S GUIDE TO LOVE AND MURDER *(Broadway 2013)*
Music by Steven Lutvak
Lyrics by Robert L. Freedman and Steven Lutvak

The musical comedy *A Gentleman's Guide to Love and Murder* is based on the 1907 novel *Israel Rank: The Autobiography of a Criminal* by Roy Horniman. The style of the light-hearted musical recalls operetta and the British music hall. The main character is Monty Navarro, a young man in London who grew up in poverty, but is informed following the death of his mother that she was a member of the noble D'Ysquith family, and that he is ninth in line to be the Earl of Highhurst. He schemes to murder those relatives who stand in his way in a series of what appear to be freak accidents. Monty is in love with Sibella, who sings **"I Don't Know What I'd Do Without You"** in Act I, after Monty informs her of his nobility. Sibella is also in love with Monty, but she will not marry him because he is poor. Instead she decides marries the likelier prospect Lionel Holland and sings **"Poor Monty."** Despite being married, Monty and Sibella carry on an affair. Monty eventually agrees to a marriage of convenience with Phoebe who sings **"I've Decided to Marry You."** Monty later becomes Lord Montague D'Ysquith Navarro, Ninth Earl of Highhurst. He is soon arrested for the one murder he didn't commit. More plot twists occur before Monty's release from prison at the end of the show.

GHOST THE MUSICAL *(London 2011; Broadway 2012)*
Music by Dave Stewart and Glen Ballard
Lyrics by Bruce Joel Rubin, Dave Stewart, and Glen Ballard

The 1990 film *Ghost*, starring Patrick Swayze, Demi Moore and Whoopi Goldberg, tells the story of Sam Wheat, a banker, and his girlfriend Molly Jensen, a sculptor, who at the beginning of the musical are moving into an apartment in Brooklyn. Sam loves Molly, but has difficulty saying it, much to Molly's disappointment. While Sam and Molly are walking home together, Sam is killed in an altercation with an armed man. Instead of crossing over to the other side, Sam remains on earth as a ghost, following Molly but unable to speak to her. With the aid of a psychic named Oda Mae, Sam solves the mystery of who was responsible for his death and saves Molly from danger. *Ghost the Musical* follows the same story as the movie. Molly sings **"With You"** near the end of Act I, while she is grieving the recent death of Sam. Near the end of Act II, she sings **"Nothing Stops Another Day"** as she tries to move on with her life.

GREY GARDENS *(Off-Broadway 2006; Broadway 2006)*
Music by Scott Frankel
Lyrics by Michael Korie

Grey Gardens the musical is based on the 1975 film documentary about an eccentric mother and her equally eccentric daughter who remain for decades in a crumbling mansion on Long Island in East Hampton, New York. After a Prologue, Act I of the musical speculates on the pasts of the principal characters as they were in July, 1941: 47-year-old mother Edith Bouvier Beale, aunt to Jacqueline Bouvier (later Kennedy Onassis), and her 21-year-old daughter Edith "Little Edie" Bouvier Beale. Their mansion home is refined and cultivated. Little Edie is in a relationship with Joseph Kennedy, Jr. (older brother of the president), but her mother sabotages the engagement. The engagement is off, but the guests are assembled for the party. Mother Edith, a singer, glosses over any trouble, instead taking center stage and performing "one of our all-time favorites," the wistful **"Will You?"** In Act II of the musical, set in 1973 and most closely based on the documentary, the 79-year-old Edith, and her 56-year-old unmarried daughter Little Edie are faded aristocrats living in filth and ruin, isolated from the world, drifting in time. Their relationship is complex and co-dependent. Edie is on the verge of leaving, she reluctantly stays and dreads **"Another Winter in a Summer Town."** Mother Edith of Act I and Little Edie of Act II are performed by the same singing actress.

THE LIGHT IN THE PIAZZA *(Broadway 2005)*
Music and Lyrics by Adam Guettel

The story, after a novella by Elizabeth Spencer, concerns a wealthy North Carolinian mother, Margaret Johnson and her beautiful, childlike 26-year-old daughter Clara on extended vacation in Florence and Rome in the summer of 1953. Soon after their arrival in Florence, through a chance encounter, Clara meets Fabrizio, a 20-year-old Italian man who speaks little English. Though there is a spark between them, Margaret protectively takes Clara away. As Clara strolls among the great art in the Uffizi Gallery, the paintings speak to her about herself, Italy, and her romantic yearnings as she sings **"The Beauty Is."** Fabrizio is determined, and with the help of his father, finally is able to spend time with Clara, though Margaret continues to attempt to discourage the romance. Margaret finally reveals the reason for her concern: because she was kicked in the head as a child by a pony, Clara has had arrested mental and emotional development. Margaret takes Clara to Rome to get her away from Fabrizio, but Clara's feelings for him remain fervent, and after much struggle she convinces her mother not to object to their marriage by singing **"The Light in the Piazza."** Other obstacles emerge. At the end of the musical, Margaret concludes that the hopeful opportunity for real love is worth any risks.

THE LITTLE MERMAID *(Broadway 2008)*
Music by Alan Menken
Lyrics by Howard Ashman and Glenn Slater

Based on the Hans Christian Andersen tale, *The Little Mermaid* became the 1989 animated Disney film musical, which was the basis for the stage musical, with several added songs. Ariel, a young, sea-dwelling mermaid, longs to be human. She falls in love with the human prince and, aided by some magic, gets her wish. Near the beginning of the show Ariel sings **"The World Above"** to express her fascination with the world where humans live and the sun shines brightly. Ursula conjures magic that allows Ariel to be human for three days, on the condition that she loses her voice. If she obtains a true love kiss from Prince Eric, she will remain human permanently. If she fails, Ursula will own Ariel's soul. Prince Eric brings the newly human Ariel back to his palace, where she is bathed and dressed by maids. Ariel, fascinated with the human world and the handsome prince, sings **"Beyond My Wildest Dreams."**

LITTLE WOMEN *(Broadway 2005)*
Music by Jason Howland
Lyrics by Mindi Dickstein

The musical is based on the famous 19th-century American novel by Louisa May Alcott about the close-knit March family of Concord, Massachusetts, during the Civil War. Four sisters (Jo, Meg, Amy, and Beth) and their mother (Marmee) make the best they can of their lives while the patriarch of the household is serving in the U.S. Army as a chaplain. Among several plot twists involving various sisters, the aspiring writer Jo lands in New York. She returns to Massachusetts when she hears that Beth, always weak, has contracted scarlet fever. As Jo attends to her dying little sister, a still cheerful and peaceful Beth sings **"Some Things Are Meant to Be"** eventually asking Jo to "let me go now." Though devastated, the family carries on after Beth's death. Amy marries Laurie, Jo's one time best friend who surprised her with a proposal she turned down. Jo matures as a young woman and a writer, and has a loving relationship with the older Professor Bhaer. The story ends with the announcement that Jo's book, *Little Women*, about her life with her sisters, has found a publisher.

A MAN OF NO IMPORTANCE *(Off-Broadway 2002)*
Music by Stephen Flaherty
Lyrics by Lynn Ahrens

A Man of No Importance is based on of the 1994 film of the same name, which starred Albert Finney. The musical won the Outer Circle Critics award for Best Off-Broadway Musical. It takes place in Dublin in 1964 and tells of Alfie Byrne, a bus conductor and director of an amateur theatre troupe that has been shut down by Father Kenny, the priest at the church where they rehearse, because he objects to their planned production of Oscar Wilde's *Salome*. Alfie's muse is Wilde, and he quotes him throughout the play. Alfie meets Adele Rice on the bus, and wants her to play the title role of the princess Salome. She sings of her astonished reaction and her modest self-perception in **"Princess."** Alfie hides his feelings for the handsome bus driver Robbie Fay, but by the end of the show he is able to face himself and who he is as a gay man.

SCHOOL OF ROCK *(Broadway 2015)*
Music by Andrew Lloyd Webber
Lyrics by Glenn Slater

The musical is based on the 2003 film. Dewey Finn loses his gig playing guitar in the band *No Vacancy*. Unemployed and with roommates demanding rent, he is desperate. Principal Rosalie Mullins from Horace Green School calls to offer a substitute teaching position to Dewey's roommate. Dewey, pretending to be the roommate, accepts the job. He shows up for his first day hungover and completely unprepared for a day of teaching. Rosalie chides him and gives him a lesson on high expectations in **"Here at Horace Green."** Dewey develops the students' musical talents in lieu of teaching other subjects. He announces that they will work up a song to perform at the Battle of the Bands. Each student takes on a unique role from costuming, to songwriting, performing, or designing lights and staging. The kids are quickly transformed from deferential learners to engaged creative thinkers. Days before the Battle of the Bands, the class finds out there is a parent's night that will conflict with the performance. Hoping to come to a compromise, Dewey asks Rosalie on a date. She loosens from her officious, cold veneer and reveals that she is a music lover in the song **"Where Did the Rock Go?"** Rosalie helps the kids get to the Battle of the Bands where they impress their families, teachers, the crowd, and themselves with their efforts.

SHREK THE MUSICAL *(Broadway 2008)*
Music by Jeanine Tesori
Lyrics by David Lindsay-Abaire

Shrek the Musical is based on the hit 2001 film, which was in turn based on William Steig's 1990 book *Shrek!* Shrek is a bitter ogre who lives as a hermit. He is disturbed from his lonely existence by a group of fairytale characters who have been exiled from their home in the Kingdom of Duloc by Lord Farquaad. Shrek goes out to reverse this order so he can have his peace and quiet back, and along the way meets Princess Fiona, who Farquaad is set on marrying. However, Shrek and Princess Fiona end up having a great deal in common, and after both friendship and fraught misunderstandings, they fall in love. **"Morning Person"** begins Act II. Princess Fiona sings the song after rising early in a chipper mood, communing with birds and animals.

TALES FROM THE BAD YEARS
Music and Lyrics by Kait Kerrigan and Brian Lowdermilk

The songwriters' synopsis from *The Kerrigan-Lowdermilk Songbook:* "The Bad Years is an immersive musical, in which audience members navigate the show for themselves and choose which characters and stories to follow. It takes place at an epic house party where we meet and follow a group of interconnected twenty-somethings through one night where they struggle to overcome an expectation of privilege in order to truly grow up. Separately, *Tales from the Bad Years* is a non-immersive song cycle of material from *The Bad Years* that can be licensed and performed in a proscenium setting. All of these songs deal with themes of coming of age in twenty-first century America. The songs stand alone are open to interpretation by any gender.... **'Not a Love Story'** is about grappling with undefined love. The character is trapped in the moment when something vivid and larger than life ends. She telescopes back in time, trying to hold onto the amorphous beauty of what was." At this writing the musical has not had an Off-Broadway production.

URINETOWN *(Broadway 2001)*
Music by Mark Hollmann
Lyrics by Mark Hollmann and Greg Kotis

Writer Greg Kotis had the seed of the idea for the show while broke in Europe and faced with a Parisian pay-per-use toilet. This helped him envision the drought-stricken world where a greedy conglomerate, Urine Good Company, owns all the toilets in a fictional city, thus making it a "Privilege to Pee." Bobby Strong helps the masses to overthrow the corrupt company, while falling for the boss's daughter Hope. She offers him advice to **"Follow Your Heart"** after Bobby's father is put in jail.

WAITRESS *(Broadway 2016)*
Music and Lyrics by Sara Bareilles

The musical is an adaptation of the 2007 independent film *Waitress*, which was written and directed by Adrienne Shelly. Waitress Jenna Hunterson is disillusioned, overworked at Joe's Pie Diner, stuck in a small southern town and unhappily married. She wants to leave her husband and open a pie shop, but becomes pregnant, complicated by an affair with a handsome doctor. At her lowest point, while pregnant, she doesn't recognize who she has become, and remembers her former, hopeful self in **"She Used to Be Mine."** Her dark mood lifts after she has a baby, and her new perspective is sung in **"Everything Changes."** In 2015 Sara Bareilles released an album of the songs written for the stage musical. Changes to some of the songs were made subsequent to the album and prior to the Broadway opening.

WICKED *(Broadway 2003; London 2006)*
Music and Lyrics by Stephen Schwartz

Based on Gregory Maguire's 1995 book, the musical chronicles the backstory of the Wicked Witch of the West, Elphaba, and Good Witch of the North, Glinda (Galinda in her youth before she changed her name), before their story threads are picked up in L. Frank Baum's *The Wonderful Wizard of Oz*. Elphaba first meets Galinda at Shiz University, where they are unlikely roommates who in the early days together clash constantly, but soon develop a close bond. Galinda gives Elphaba a new nickname, Elphie, and vows to help her become **"Popular."** Elphaba unjustly gets labeled as "wicked," While Galinda (now Glinda after her name change) is perceived as the good and smiling representative of the Wizard of Oz, who is actually an evil fake. Both Glinda and Elphaba want the prince Fiyero, but he loves Elphaba. Elphaba stages a false death. Fiyero (now a scarecrow due to a spell) and Elphaba are happily reunited. The Wizard (actually Elphaba's father) is exiled from Oz by Glinda, who promises to earn her title as Glinda the Good.

YOUNG FRANKENSTEIN *(Broadway 2007)*
Music and Lyrics by Mel Brooks

Following the success of the 2001 musical adaptation of his film *The Producers*, Mel Brooks started work on a musical version of *Young Frankenstein*, based on his 1974 movie spoof on horror films. The plot, set in the 1930s, follows Frederick Frankenstein, a scientist in New York who is ashamed of his family name and heritage. After the death of his mad scientist grandfather in Transylvania, Frederick travels there to see a castle he has inherited. He soon takes over his grandfather's project, bringing a monster that he had created to life. He is met in Transylvania by his grandfather's henchman, Igor, and the lovely yodeling lab assistant that Igor has hired for him, Inga. She sings **"Listen to Your Heart"** to Frederick at the beginning of Act II, as she tries to soothe Frederick after the monster has run away.

WAITING
from *The Addams Family*

Music and Lyrics by
Andrew Lippa

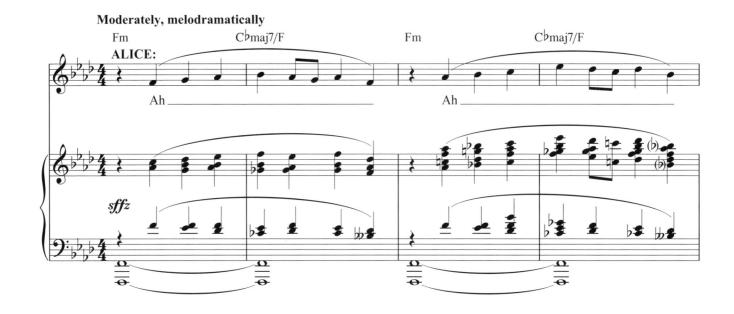

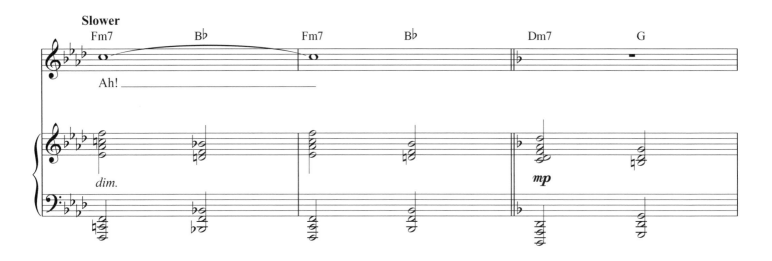

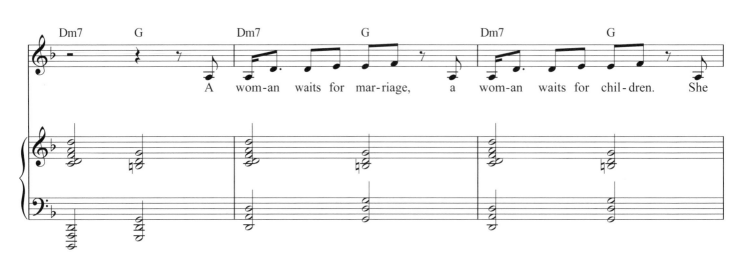

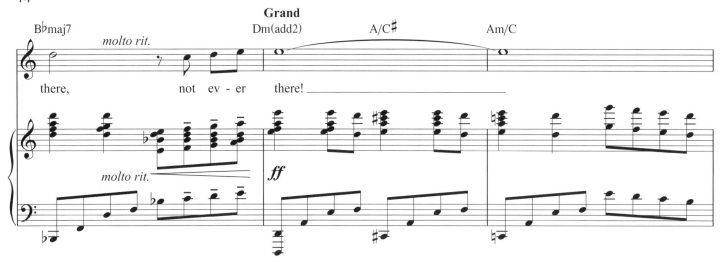

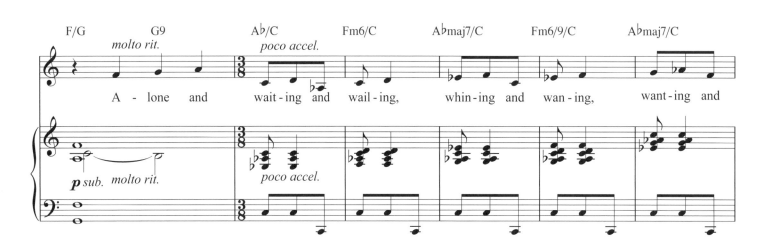

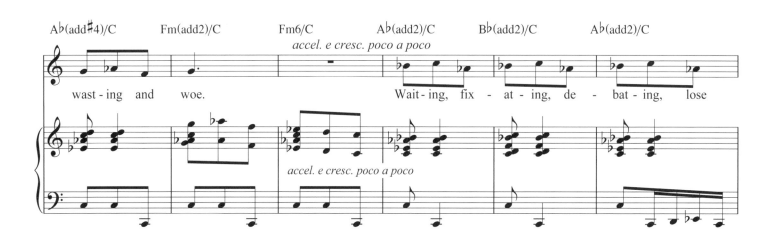

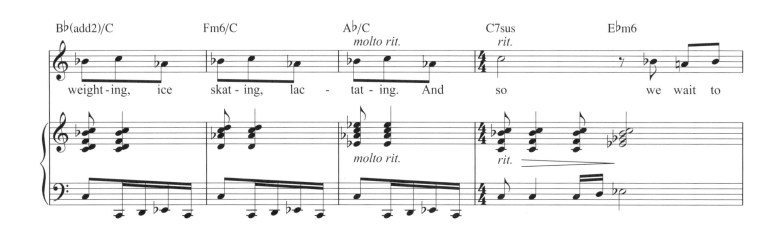

TELL ME WHY
from *Amazing Grace*

Music and Lyrics by Christopher Smith

I STILL BELIEVE
from *Amazing Grace*

Music and Lyrics by Christopher Smith

TWO MEN IN MY LIFE
from *Big Fish*

Music and Lyrics by
Andrew Lippa

let the man_ a - muse_ you?_____ He tells a harm-less

tale that al-ways drives you mad. But aren't you tell-ing

sto - ries too, your point of view just dif-f'rent from your dad. There are

two men in_ my life:_ him and you._ And the

sto - ries I be - lieve_ in all__ come true.__ He can

give you what you need,_ but you should take the lead._

rit.

_ There is mag - ic in the man, please

colla voce

a tempo *rit.*

find it while you can._____

I DON'T NEED A ROOF

from *Big Fish*

Music and Lyrics by
Andrew Lippa

Simply, vocal rhythm not strict

SANDRA:

In your face I see a life-time.

In this place I feel at ease.

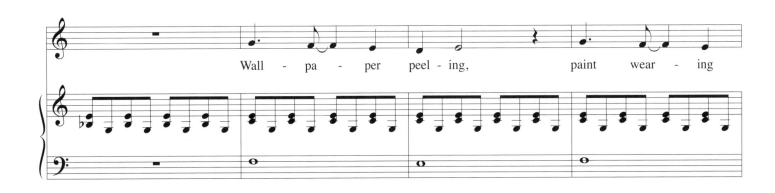

Wall - pa - per peel - ing, paint wear - ing

thin. Here's where__ I end and__ be - gin.

TO BUILD A HOME
from the Broadway Musical *The Bridges of Madison County*

Music and Lyrics by
Jason Robert Brown

Chaconne, poco rubato, in 1 (♩ = 155)

rall.   **FRANCESCA:**

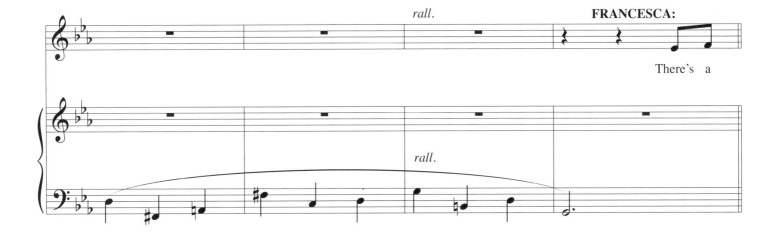

There's a

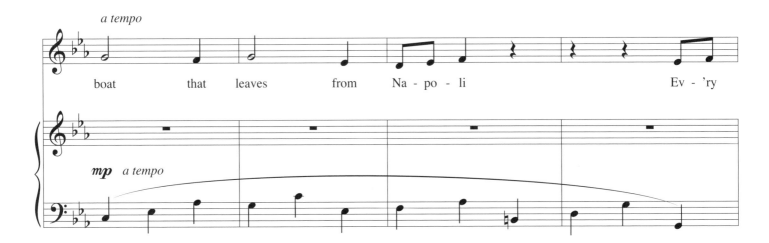

boat   that   leaves   from   Na - po - li   Ev - 'ry

40

44

Gm/C

hearts she used to break,_____ the

Gm7(♭5)/C

lies she used to tell,_____ and the

F/C   C7sus   *poco rall.*

wom - an she grew up_____ to

poco rall.

A tempo (quasi 6/8-feel) (♩. = 68)

F2

be._____

ff *r.h.*   *l.h.*

WHAT DO YOU CALL
A MAN LIKE THAT?

from The Bridges of Madison County

Music and Lyrics by
Jason Robert Brown

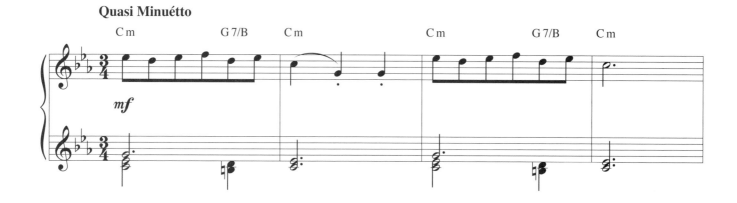

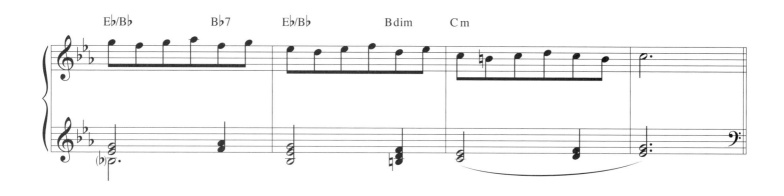

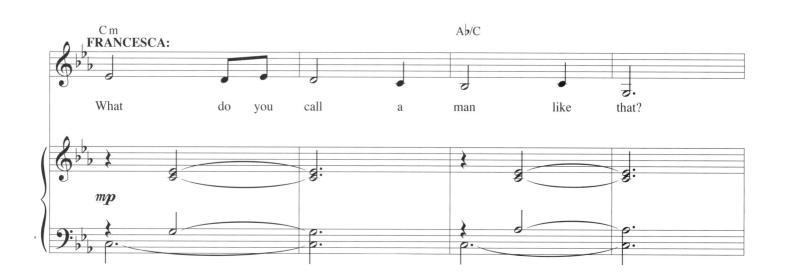

62

ALWAYS BETTER

from the Broadway Musical *The Bridges of Madison County*

Music and Lyrics by
Jason Robert Brown

THE VIEW FROM HERE

from *Darling*

Music and Lyrics by
Ryan Scott Oliver

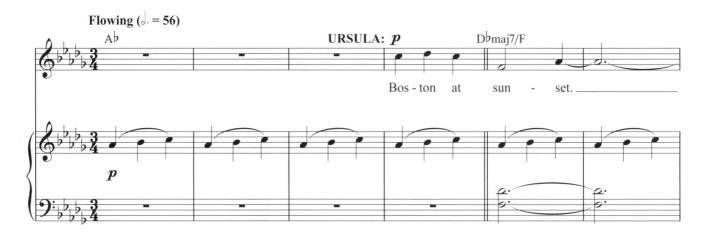

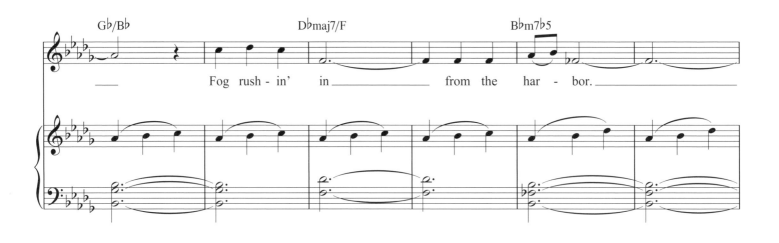

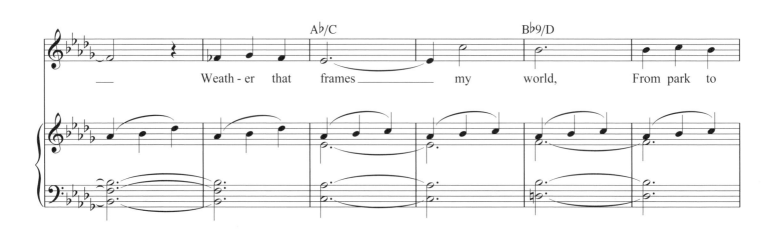

NOTHING IS TOO WONDERFUL TO BE TRUE

from *Dirty Rotten Scoundrels*

Words and Music by
David Yazbek

This song is a duet between Christine and Freddy, adapted here as a solo. A reprise of the song in the show has been incorporated into this edition.

true. If I'm per-ceived to be na-ïve to be the way

I am, let peo-ple say I am a sil-ly goof. Is life a

plate-ful? Am I grate-ful? Ev-'ry day I am. It's an a-maz-

-ing world in which we live and I've got liv-in' proof.

I REMEMBER

from *Ever After*

Lyrics by Marcy Heisler
Music by Zina Goldrich

HEAVEN KNOWS

from *Far from Heaven*

Music by Scott Frankel
Lyrics by Michael Korie

more a per - son grows, as heav - en on - ly

knows. All the same, some - how I see

Poco più mosso

agitato

be-yond the shell of my co - coon, the trem-bling of a but - ter - fly to -

poco rall.

dolce
poco rall.

be... And al - though the world is wide, I'll

a tempo

sub. **mp**

cresc.

find my stride which - ev - er way the side - walk goes.

Un - til I'm

rall.

a tempo - agitato

there,

don't ask me where each ap - ple blos - som blows. _____

rall.

a tempo

a tempo - agitato
molto espressivo

rall.

fp

a tempo

rall.

a tempo

The an - swer is... who knows?

mp

fp *a tempo*

With some Rubato (in 4)

A pic - ture post - card with an

p espressivo

ear - ly spring New Eng - land theme, though now it's

dolce

not as close to heav - en as it used to seem.

rall.

mp

rall.

accel. poco a poco

That was just a _____ dream... _____

mp

molto cresc. poco a poco

rall.

rall.

f

ALL THAT MATTERS

from *Finding Neverland*

Words and Music by
Elliot Kennedy and Gary Barlow

98

SYLVIA'S LULLABY

from *Finding Neverland*

Words and Music by Eliot Kennedy
and Gary Barlow

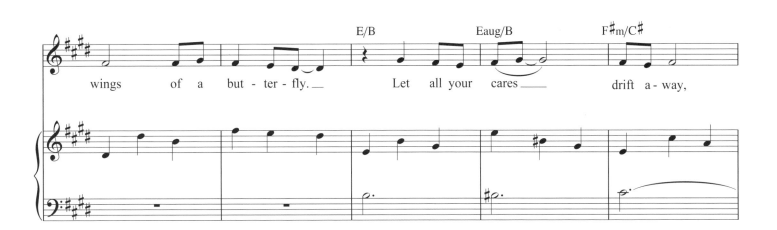

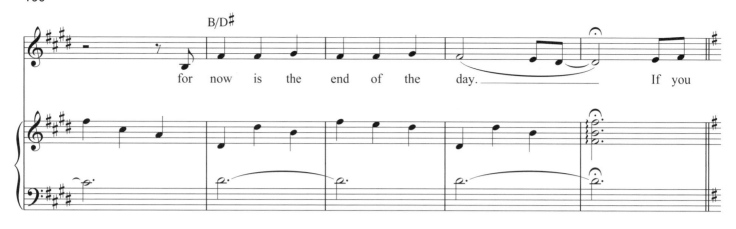

for now is the end of the day. _____ If you

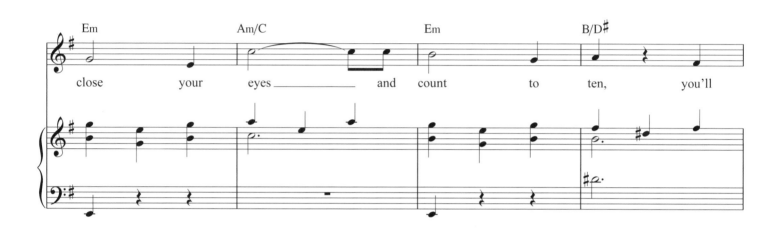

close your eyes _____ and count to ten, you'll

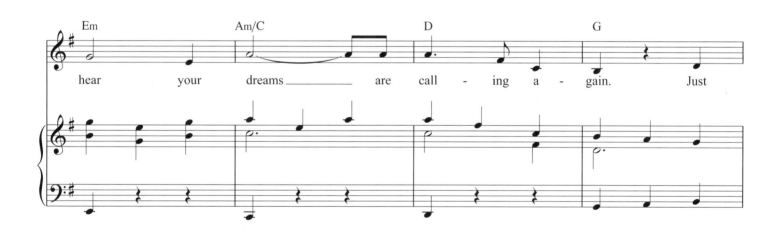

hear your dreams _____ are call - ing a - gain. Just

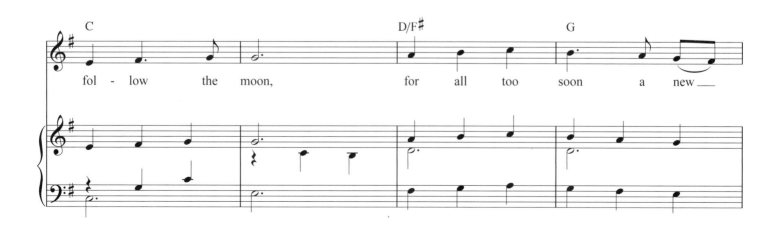

fol - low the moon, for all too soon a new ___

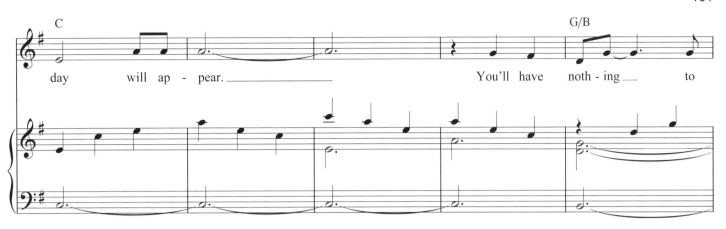

day will ap - pear.____ You'll have noth - ing __ to

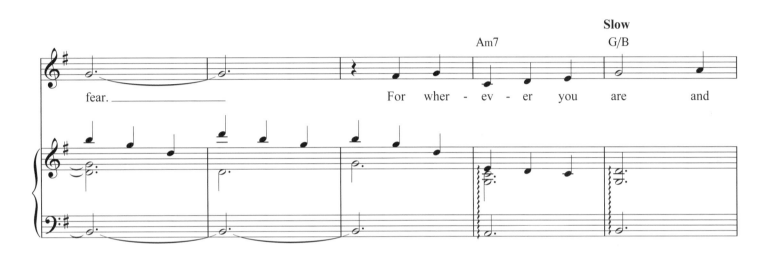

fear.____ For wher - ev - er you are and

for - ev - er __ I'll be here.____

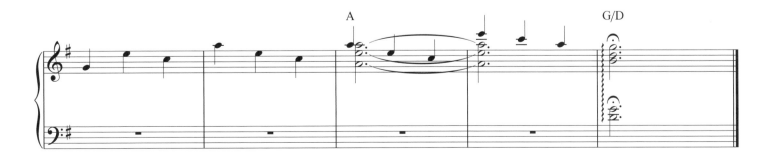

I DON'T KNOW WHAT I'D DO WITHOUT YOU

from *A Gentleman's Guide to Love and Murder*

Music by Steven Lutvak
Lyrics by Robert L. Freedman
and Steven Lutvak

POOR MONTY

from *A Gentleman's Guide to Love and Murder*

Music by Steven Lutvak
Lyrics by Robert L. Freedman and
Steven Lutvak

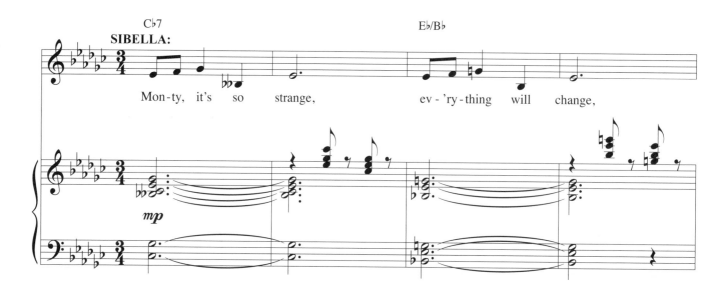

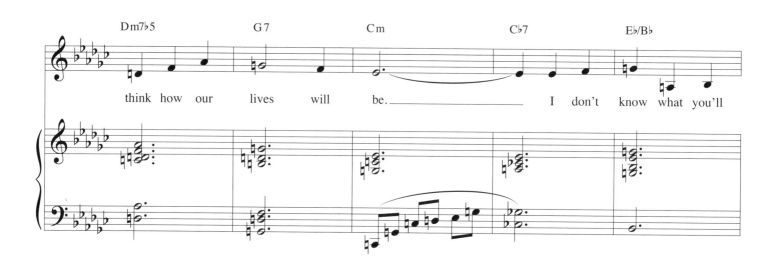

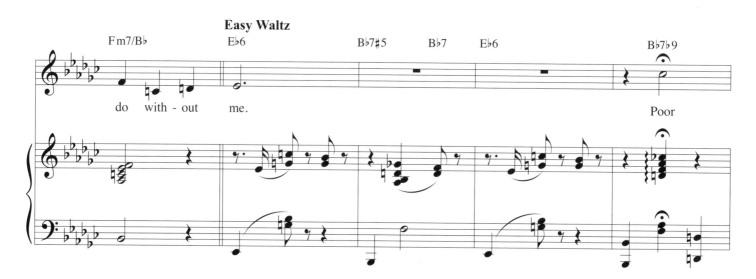

SIBELLA:

I can pic-ture us now, ver-y grand, in de-mand, al-ways some-where ex-cit-ing to go! All of May-fair will im-i-tate us, love us, and hate us for be-ing the peo-ple peo-ple want to know! My

* Later. At her wedding. She sings of her husband-to-be.

I'VE DECIDED TO MARRY YOU
(Solo Opening Section)*
from *A Gentleman's Guide to Love and Murder*

Music by Steven Lutvak
Lyrics by Robert L. Freedman
and Steven Lutvak

Mis-ter Na-var - ro! For - give my in-tru - sion! I

need-ed to see you, and see you to - day!

*The song becomes a trio for Phoebe, Sibella and Monty. This is the opening solo section.

HOW WILL I KNOW?
from *Death Takes a Holiday*

Music and Lyrics by
Maury Yeston

WITH YOU
from *Ghost the Musical*

Words and Music by Glen Ballard,
David Allan Stewart and Bruce Joel Rubin

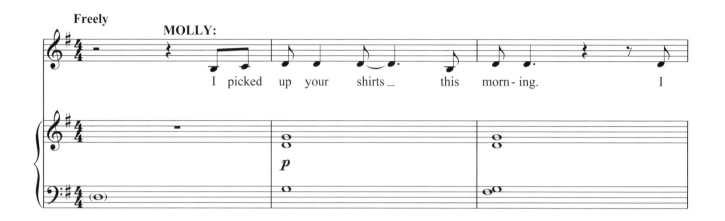

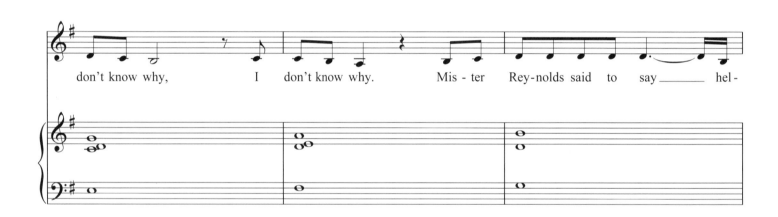

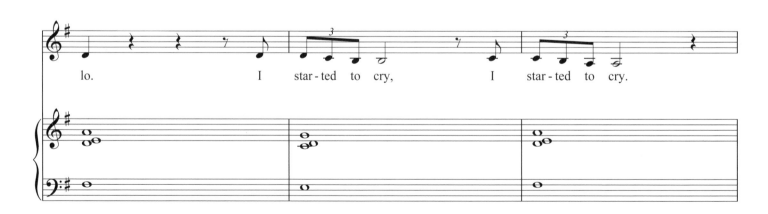

Più mosso

Ev - 'ry place __ we ev - er walked __ and ev - 'ry-where __ we talked, __

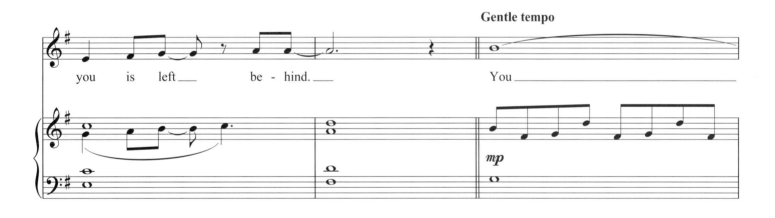

__ I miss you. You nev - er leave __ my mind, So much __ of

Gentle tempo

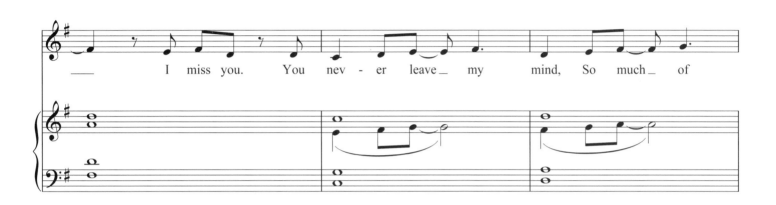

you is left __ be - hind. __ You __

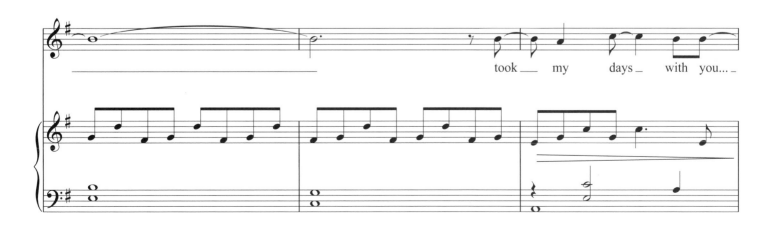

__ took __ my days __ with you.... __

feel-ings of __ re-gret. __ I can't com - pre - hend this, _____ and pre-tend __

__ that I ____ don't care. __ An - y place __ I _____

want to be __ I want __ to see __ you there. _____

più cresc.

You _____

pp

NOTHING STOPS ANOTHER DAY

from *Ghost the Musical*

Words and Music by Glen Ballard,
David Allan Stewart and Bruce Joel Rubin

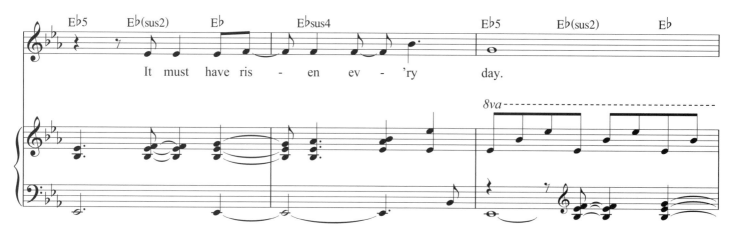

WILL YOU?

from *Grey Gardens*

Music by Scott Frankel
Lyrics by Michael Korie

EDITH: *Good afternoon everyone, and welcome*

to Grey Gardens. I'd like to commence our little tribute to young love with one of our all-time favorites. Gould?—"Will You?"

When

li - lacs re - turn in spring, will you? _____ When

If the dialogue is omitted at the beginning, the song may be started at the Cantabile tempo. "Gould" is a reference to a musician.

larks in the mea - dow sing, will you? _____ When

clouds of a sum-mer storm dis-solve and star - light shim-mers through, will

poco rall.

Poco più mosso

you? _____ When

mf espressivo

rall.

dim.

rall.

Tempo I

wild geese of au - tumn fly, will you? _____ When

mp

148

hearth fires of win - ter die, will you?

Time rush - es by, mem - o - ries fade. Dreams nev - er do.

cresc.

dolce

dim.

Poco più mosso

I will be ev - er true... will you?

espressivo

Edie's going to be tickled pink to see you all here.   *I'm afraid she's slipped away for the moment.*

*

* *If the dialogue is omitted, a possible cut may be made from * to **.*

ANOTHER WINTER
IN A SUMMER TOWN

from *Grey Gardens*

Music by Scott Frankel
Lyrics by Michael Korie

Brief sections of the song are a duet for Edie and Edith, edited here as a solo for Edie.

crown. From blos-som to blos-som, I buzz like a bee. ___ Then

Slower

glance in the mir - ror, and who do I see? __ A mid - dle - aged wom - an in -

ten. *poco agitato*

hab - it-ing me __ be-cause it's win - ter ___ in a sum-mer town.

poco agitato

rall. *a tempo*

Hmm __ hmm ___ la da da da da

rall. *colla voce* *a tempo*

con pedale

Da da da da da da da da   Ah _____ ah _____

dim.   *agitato*

poco più mosso

Yes-ter-day's dreams,   a   fa-ded bou-quet   Ros-es that died   on the

poco più mosso

vine.   Yes-ter-day seems _____ more real than to-day.

cresc.

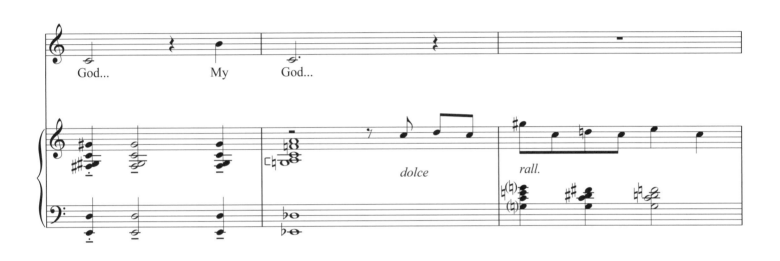

SOME THINGS ARE MEANT TO BE

from the Stage Musical *Little Women*

Music by Jason Howland
Lyrics by Mindi Dickstein

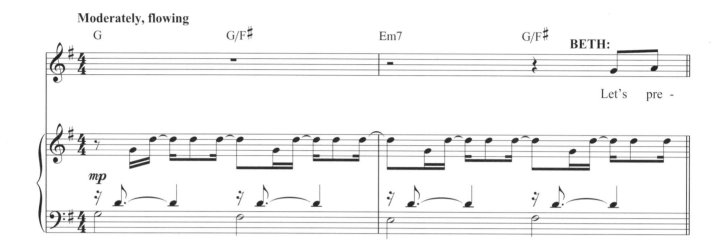

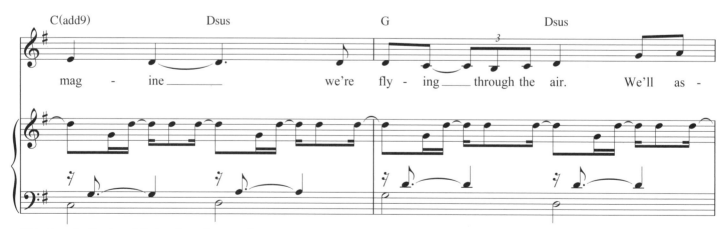

This duet for Beth and Jo is adapted as a solo.

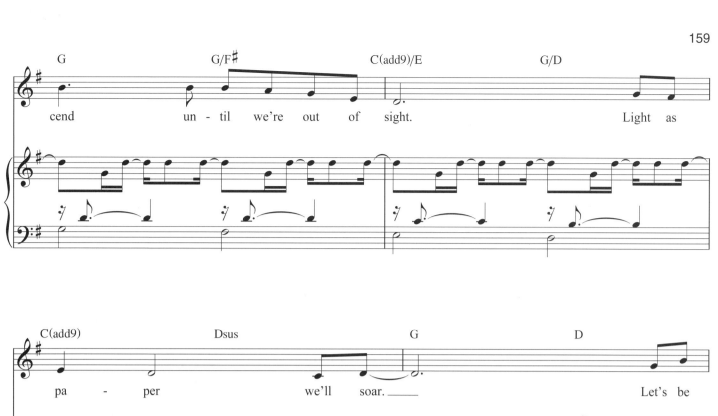

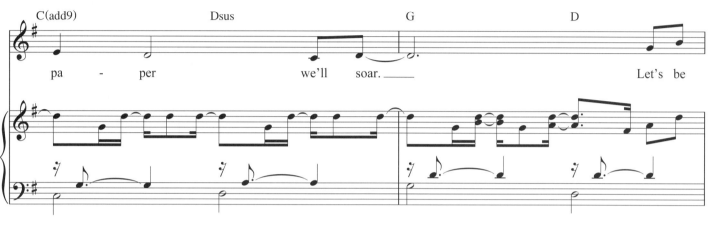

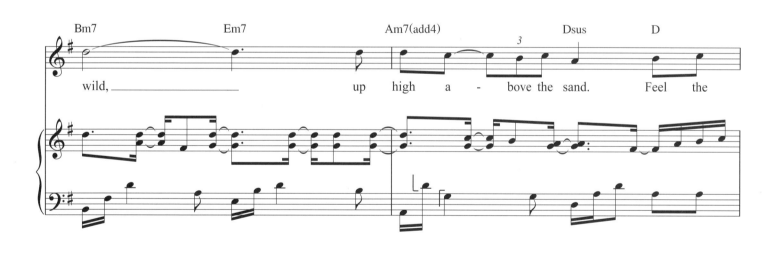

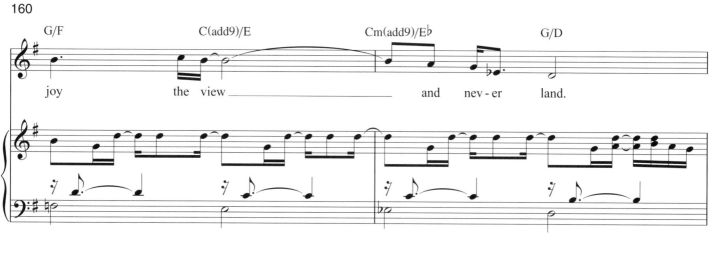

joy   the view _____ and nev - er land.

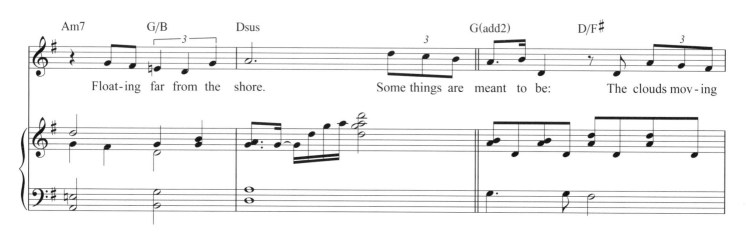

Float-ing far from the shore.   Some things are meant to be: The clouds mov-ing

fast   and free.   The sun on a sil - ver sea.   A

sky that's bright and blue. And some things will nev - er end: The thrill of our

nev - er die: the prom-ise of who you are, your mem-'ries when I am far from

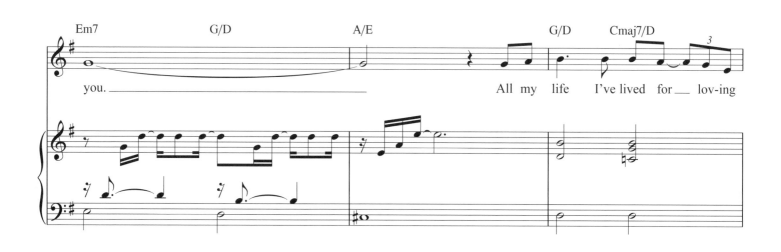

you. _____ All my life I've lived for __ lov-ing

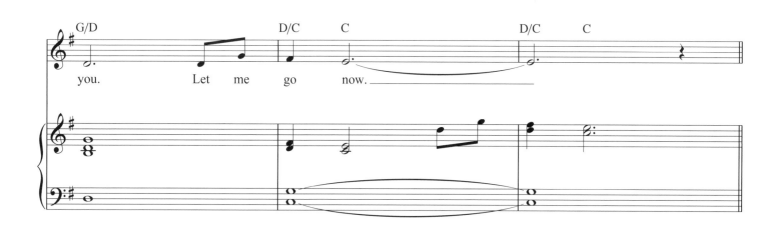

you. Let me go now. _____

Tempo I

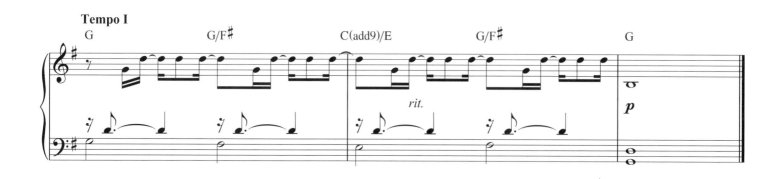

THE BEAUTY IS
from *The Light in the Piazza*

Words and Music by
Adam Guettel

With a strong pulse

CLARA:

These are ver - y pop - u - lar in It - a - ly!

It's the land of na - ked mar - ble boys! ___

Some - thing we don't see a lot in Win - ston Sa - lem.

That's the land of cor - du - roys! ___

Poco più mosso, flowing, but exact tempo

I'm just a some-one in an

mf

old mu - se - um. Far a - way from home as some-one can go.

And the beau - ty is I still meet peo - ple I know. ___ Hel -

Expressively

lo. This is want-ing some-thing. This is reach-ing for it.

mp

This is wish-ing that a mo-ment would ar - rive. This is tak - ing chanc - es.

hard - ly met a sin - gle soul, but I am not a - lone._____ I feel

accel. poco a poco

p

accel. poco a poco

Tempo II (Poco più mosso)

known! This is want-ing some-thing. This is pray-ing for it.

f

This is hold-ing breath and keep-ing fin - gers crossed. This is count-ing bless-ings.

This is won-d'ring when I'll see that__ boy a - gain. __

THE LIGHT IN THE PIAZZA

from *The Light in the Piazza*

Words and Music by
Adam Guettel

Con moto (in 2)

CLARA:

I don't see a mir-a-cle shin-ing from the sky.

I'm no good at stat-ues and sto-ries. I try.

That's not what I think a-bout. That's not what I see.

174

ev - 'ry - where! Fa - bri - zi - o.
7
3
mf
8vb
The light in the piazza. My love.
mp

POPULAR
from the Broadway Musical *Wicked*

Music and Lyrics by
Stephen Schwartz

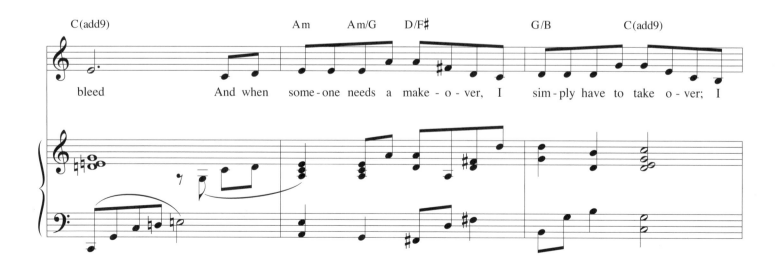

THE WORLD ABOVE

from Walt Disney's *The Little Mermaid – A Broadway Musical*

Music by Alan Menken
Lyrics by Glenn Slater

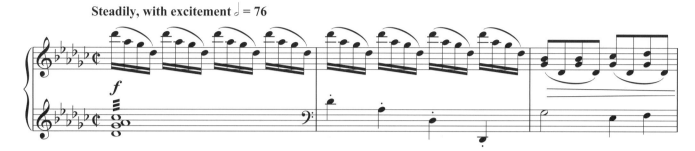

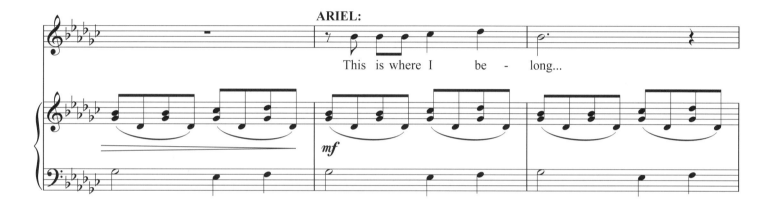

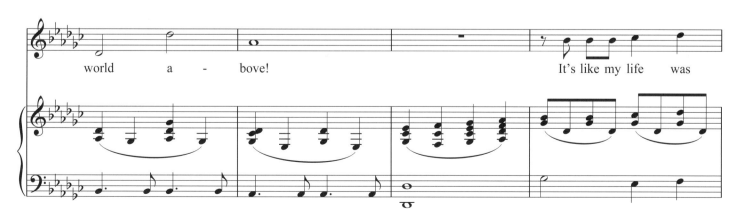

wrong. And some-how, now, at last I'm in

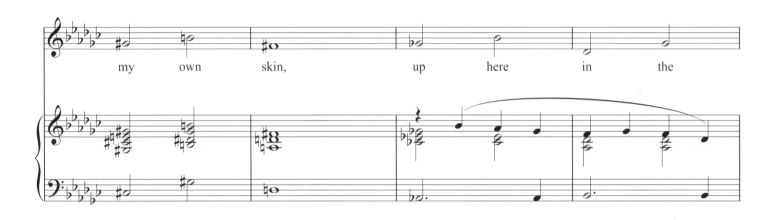

my own skin, up here in the

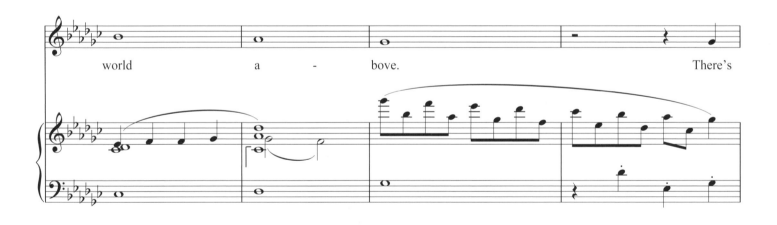

world a - bove. There's

so much light here, light and space. The

legato

sun's so bright here, up - on my _____ face. It

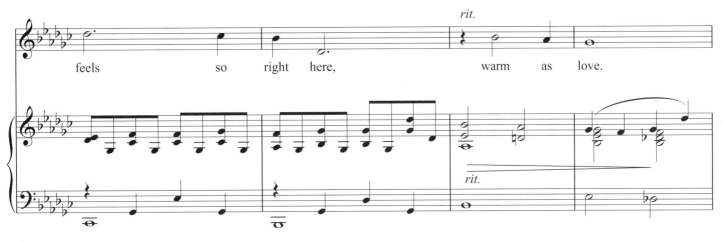

feels so right here, warm as love.

rit.

Freely

Life seems to be al - most call - ing to me from this strange new world a -

a tempo

bove.

a tempo   *poco rit.*

BEYOND MY WILDEST DREAMS

from Walt Disney's *The Little Mermaid – A Broadway Musical*

Music by Alan Menken
Lyrics by Glenn Slater

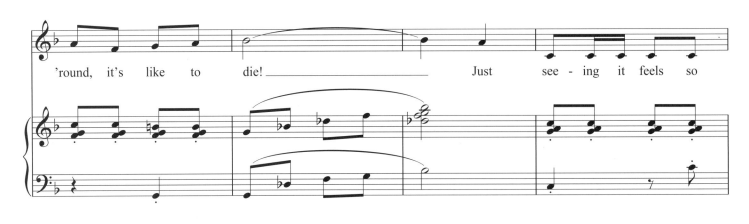

'round, it's like to die! _____ Just see-ing it feels so

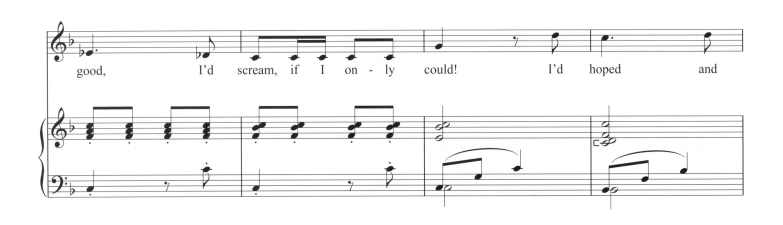

good, I'd scream, if I on-ly could! I'd hoped and

wished and want-ed so to be here. Wished and prayed and

planned it to a T. Prayed, and wow! Just look, it's real-ly

me here! Walk - ing a - round, strange as it seems, some - where be - yond my

wild - est dreams!

I'd hoped and wished and won - dered what I'd

do here. Wished and prayed and pic-tured what I'd see.

Prayed, and wow! My pray'rs are com-ing true here.

Look at it all, look how it gleams! Love-ly be-yond my wild-est

dreams.

Look, it's him! So hand-some and re-fined and slim. Sweet, sin-cere, mag - nif - i - cent from head to toe. And oh, I'd hoped and wished my life would feel en-

poco rit.

Meno mosso

PRINCESS

from *A Man of No Importance*

Words by Lynn Ahrens
Music by Stephen Flaherty

Moderately fast folk (♩ = 92)

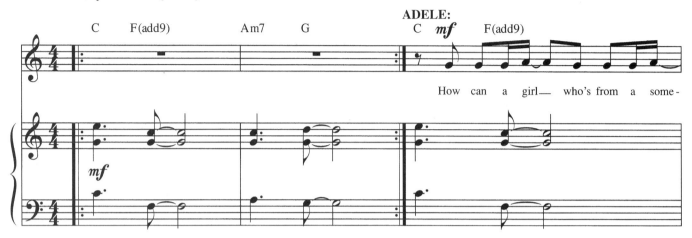

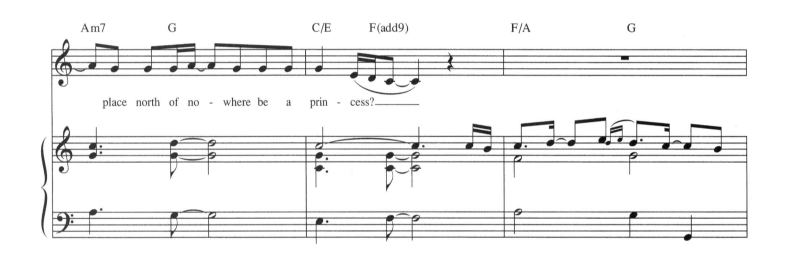

HERE AT HORACE GREEN

from *School of Rock*

Music by Andrew Lloyd Webber
Lyrics by Glenn Slater

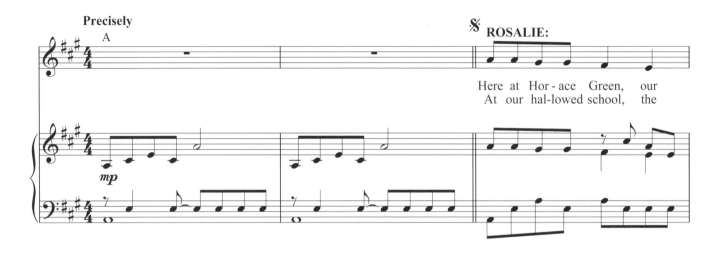

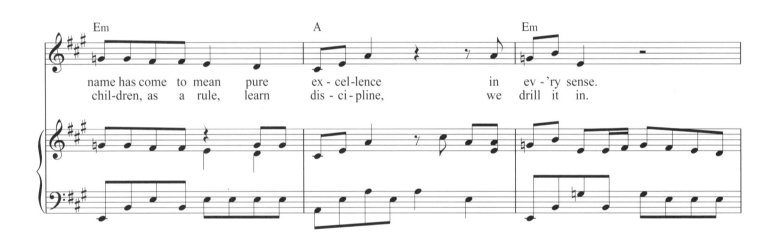

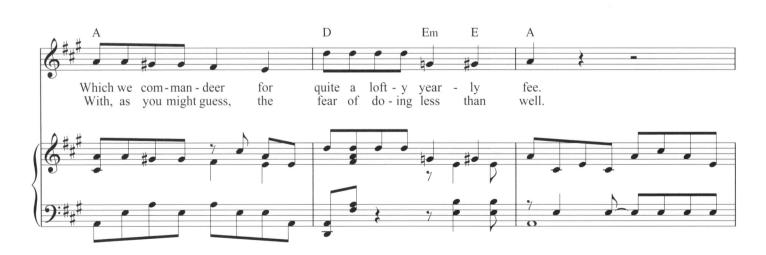

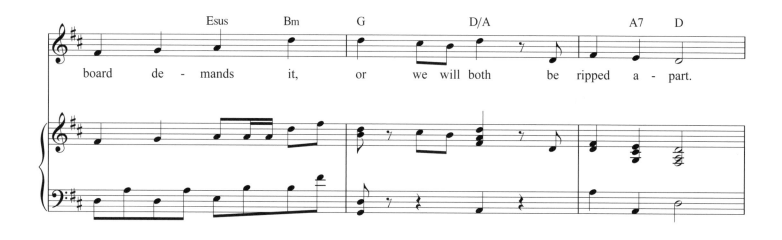

board de - mands it, or we will both be ripped a - part.

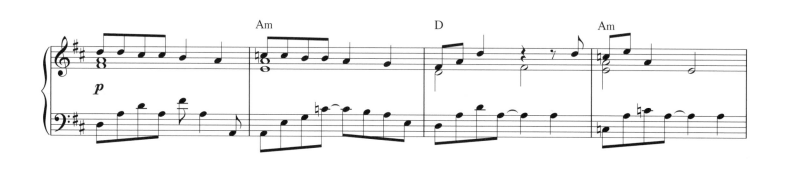

D.S. al Coda

CODA

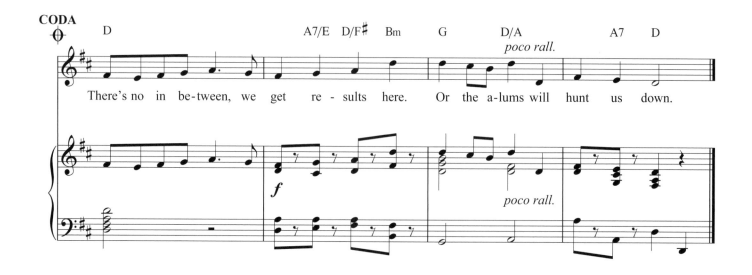

There's no in be - tween, we get re - sults here. Or the a - lums will hunt us down.

WHERE DID THE ROCK GO?

from *School of Rock*

Music by Andrew Lloyd Webber
Lyrics by Glenn Slater

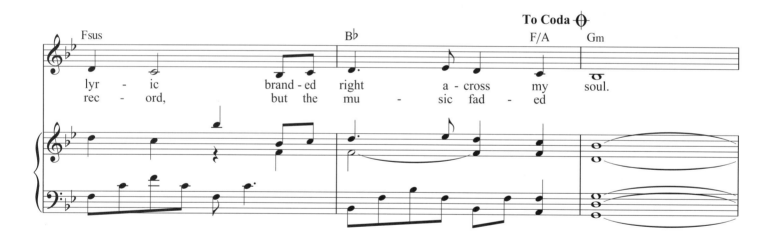

did the time go? Where's the joy I used to

know way back when? Where's the pow - er and the beau -

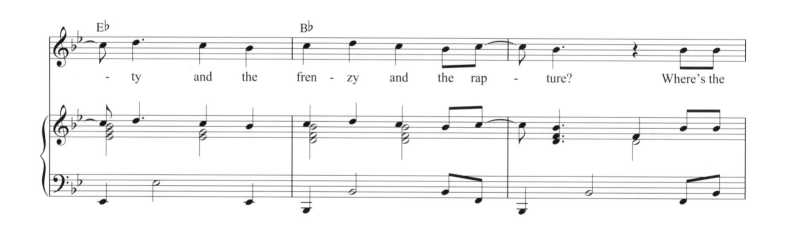

- ty and the fren - zy and the rap - ture? Where's the

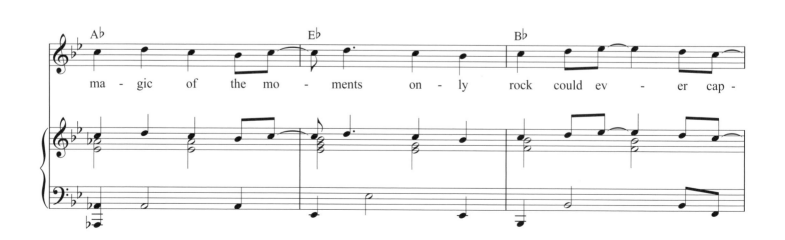

ma - gic of the mo - ments on - ly rock could ev - er cap -

MORNING PERSON
from *Shrek the Musical*

Words and Music by Jeanine Tesori
and David Lindsay-Abaire

NOT A LOVE STORY

from *Tales from the Bad Years*

Words and Music by
Kait Kerrigan
and Brian Lowdermilk

Moderately, with passion ($\quad$ = 108)

It's not a

love sto - ry. It's not a com - ing of _____ age. _____

It's not the kind of thing _____ you put in - to a

224

FOLLOW YOUR HEART
from *Urinetown*

Music and Lyrics by Mark Hollmann
Book and Lyrics by Greg Kotis

This song is a duet for Hope and Bobby in the show, adapted here as a solo.

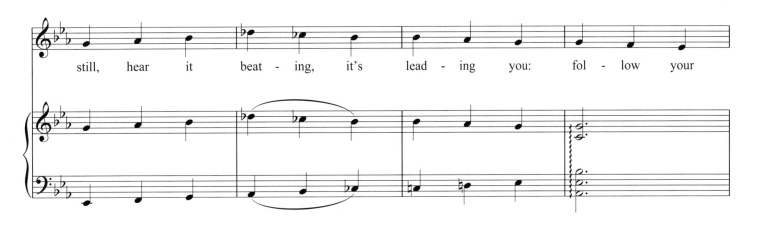

still, hear it beat - ing, it's lead - ing you: fol - low your

heart. _____

rit.   *a tempo*

We all want a world filled with peace and with

mp

joy, with plen - ty of wa - ter for each girl and

boy. That bright, shin - ing world is just wait - ing to

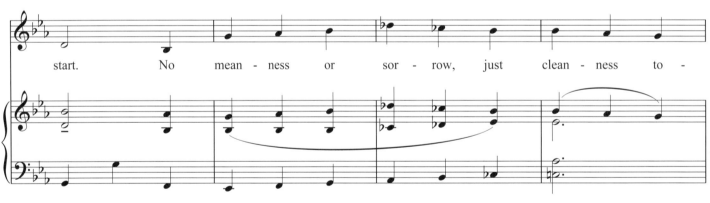

start. No mean - ness or sor - row, just clean - ness to -

mor - row, if on - ly you fol - low your heart.

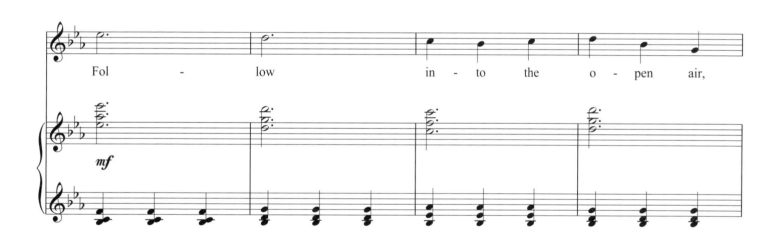

Fol - low into the o - pen air,

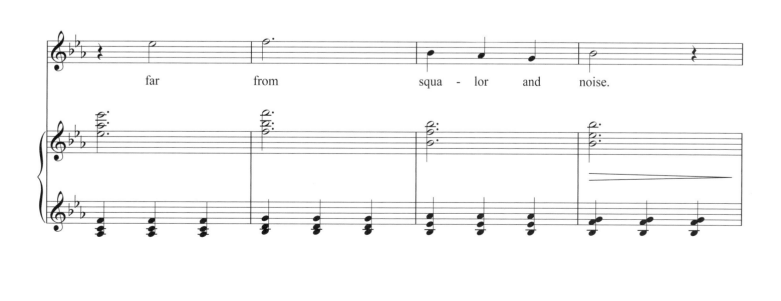

far from squa - lor and noise.

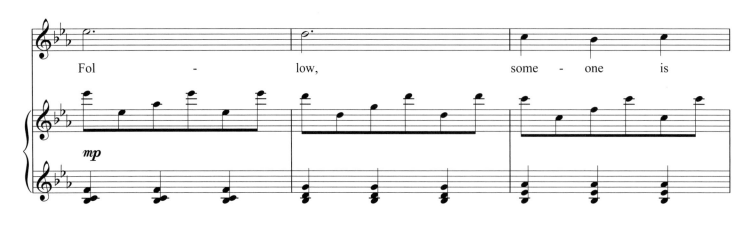

Fol - low, some - one is

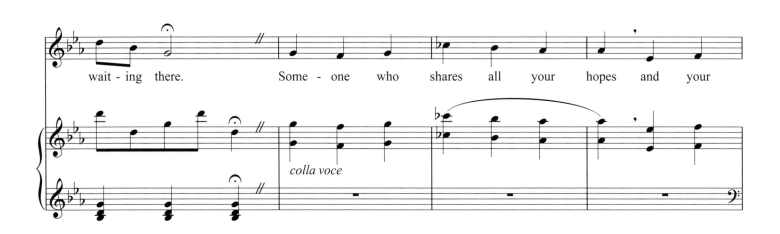

wait - ing there. Some - one who shares all your hopes and your

colla voce

a tempo

joys. Some day I'll meet

a tempo

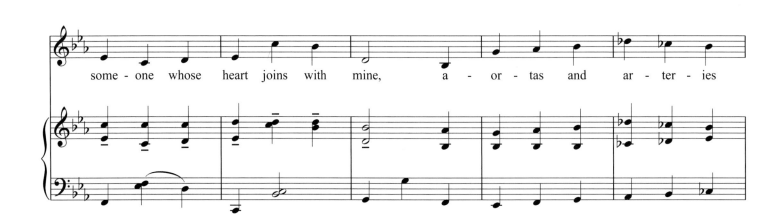

some - one whose heart joins with mine, a - or - tas and ar - ter - ies

all in - ter - twined. They'll beat so much strong - er than

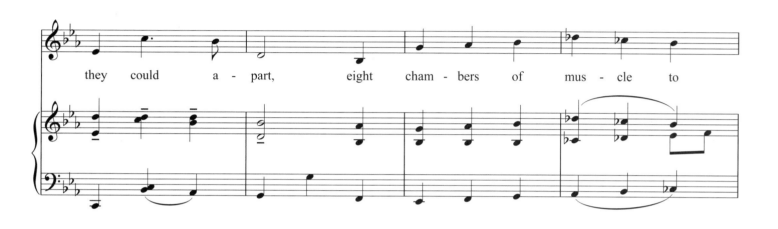

they could a - part, eight cham - bers of mus - cle to

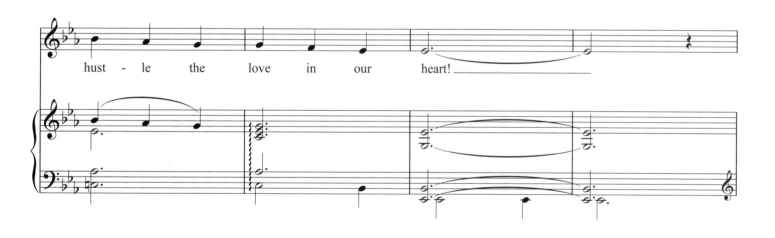

hust - le the love in our heart!

Love is kind and con - si - der - ate,

mf

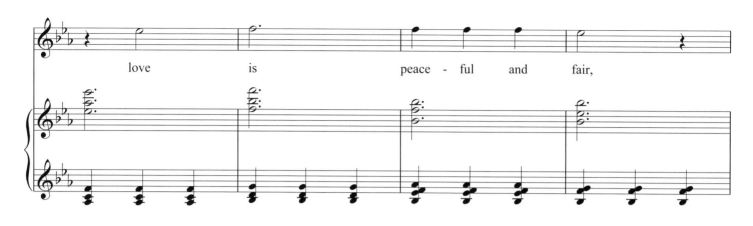

love   is   peace - ful   and   fair,

Love   can   creep up   so   sud - den - ly;

poco rit.

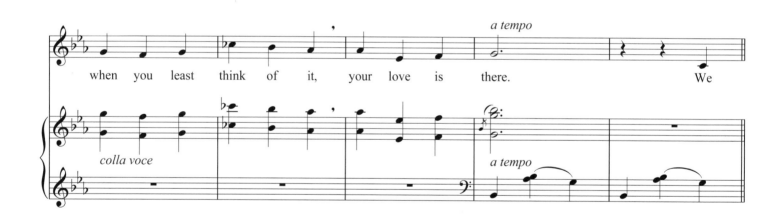

when   you   least   think   of   it,   your   love   is   there.   We

a tempo

colla voce

all   want   a   world   filled   with   peace   and   with   joy,   with   plen - ty   of

f

SHE USED TO BE MINE
from *Waitress the Musical*

Words and Music by
Sara Bareilles

EVERYTHING CHANGES
from *Waitress the Musical*

Words and Music by
Sara Bareilles

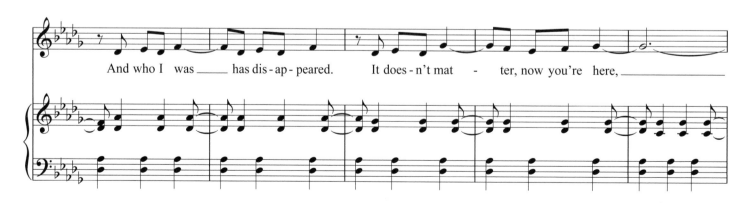

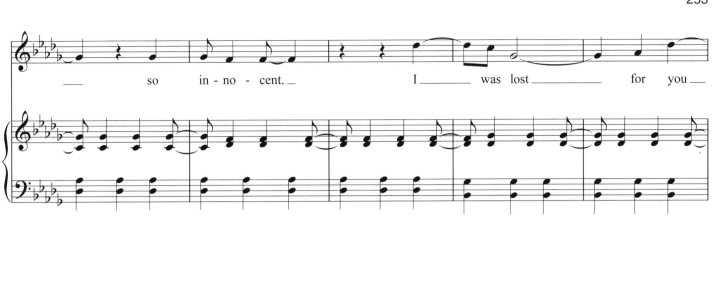

so in - no - cent. __ I __ was lost __ for you __

__ to find, now __ I'm yours __ and you __ are mine. __

Two ti - ny hands, __ a pair of eyes, an un - sung mel - o - dy is mine __

for safe - keep - ing. __ And I will guard __ it with my life.

I'd hang the moon __ for it to shine _____ on her sleep - ing. __

Start - ing here _____ and start - ing now, I __

__ can feel _____ the heart __ of how _____ ev - 'ry-thing chang -

Well, my heart's at the wheel_____ now,_____ and__ all my__ mis - takes,_____ they make sense when__ I turn them a - round.__ Ev - 'ry - thing chang - es. What I thought was__ so per - ma - nent

fades. _____ In the blink of ___ an eye _____ there's a

new life ___ in front of ___ my face. _____

And we know in ___ due time ev - 'ry

right thing ___ will find it's ___ right place. _____

LISTEN TO YOUR HEART

from *Young Frankenstein*

Music and Lyrics by
Mel Brooks

1930s Cole Porter Beguine, not too fast

INGA:
Let's for-get __ a-bout think __ -ing.

Think-ing's nev-er smart. Flush your brain __ right

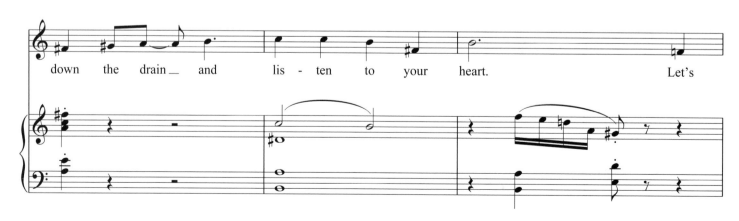

down the drain __ and lis-ten to your heart. Let's

heart. As ev - 'ry - bod - y knows, if it's

sex they're think - ing of, in - tel - lec - tu - als ____ are in - ef - fec - tu - als when it

comes to mak - ing love. Nietz - sche al - ways said he

would - n't. ____ Scho - pen - hau - er thought he should - n't. ____ And

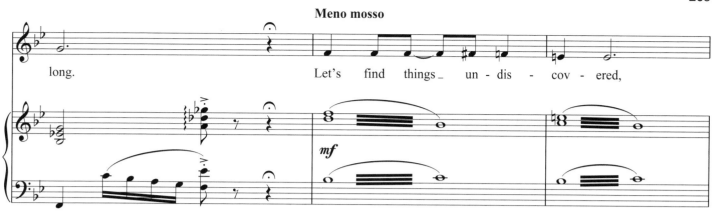

Meno mosso

long. Let's find things __ un - dis - cov - ered,

don't re - sist __ Cu - pid's dart.

Soft & seductively

You'll find such joy __ just in

mf

colla voce

be - ing a boy, so lis - ten, _____ lis - ten to your

p

heart. _____